SAVING MONEY USING COUPONS

Sharon L. Johnson, Coupon Instructor

DEDICATION

This book is dedicated to God for giving me the inspiration and motivation to proceed with one of my heart's desires. Moreover, He has given me the tenacity, courage and ability to share this information with you and for this I am very grateful.

It is dedicated to my dearest Mom, the late Ms. Arnita D. Tucker, who always encouraged me to be my best, do my best, and act accordingly. She was my hero! She was the greatest mom ever! I sincerely know that she would be extremely proud of this accomplishment...Love FOREVER. I also dedicate this book to the best son in the world, Jamaal. I love you, Son. It's a pleasure to be your Mom.

Last, but, certainly not least, I dedicate this work to YOU. Many of you have taken my classes and have gleaned from me what it takes to be an effective "couponer." Hopefully, as you read and learn more, you will become better at using coupons as a means of saving money.

Happy couponing!

INTRODUCTION

WELCOME to Saving Money Using Coupons. By reading this book and employing the strategies listed herein, you are taking giant steps towards becoming proficient and effective at couponing! Yes, by using these strategies, you will beyond any doubt save lots of money! As stated many times throughout this book, couponing requires time, patience, organization, and hard work. Of those four requirements, organization is bulls-eye! If you can manage to stay organized, then you will probably flourish, save many dollars and reap great success (in due time).

Think about this for a moment. If it was too easy then more people would be doing it. Most of us would love to have the opportunities for greater savings come to us! (smile) I assure you that the big savings will begin after reading this book and employing what you have learned. You will advance in your couponing results and be on the cutting edge towards achieving greater savings. Personally, I have learned to employ these strategies through research, hard work, dedication, determination and commitment. Because I have gone through trial and error, and moved forward with persistence to succeed, I am now able to share this information to encourage you as you explore and begin to master the "art" of couponing. To me, couponing is lots of fun and you really can save lots of money using them.

Sharon L. Johnson

CONTENTS

SPECIAL THANKS

I would like to thank my pastor Bishop Darren L. Gay, Sr., for sharing with me a broader "life" and "depth" of God. Bishop has always inspired me to aim high in God. Thusly, I have grown in faith, commitment, dedication and love for God...thanks Bishop.

Thanks to Karen R. Winston, author, who literally provoked me into this book. Every Sunday she would say to me "the book." Karen pushed me until something happened. She demolished my procrastination spirit (smile). Thanks a million, Karen.

Thanks to Eddie Worrell, who assisted me in correcting this work. In spite of his very busy schedule, he graciously found time to assist me—thanks Elder Worrell.

ACKNOWLEDGMENTS

In these hard economic times, people are searching for innovative ways to shop, save money and be less stressed. As the community of couponers grows, I happily acknowledge the input and participation of all those who have attended and who will attend my couponing workshops in the future. Together, we will make shopping a more affordable and less expensive reality.

Sharon L. Johnson

CHAPTER ONE
ORIGIN OF A COUPON

According to Wikipedia, in 1887, the Coca-Cola Company was incorporated in Atlanta, GA. Asa Candler, one of the partners, transformed Coca-Cola from an insignificant tonic into a profitable business by using innovative advertising techniques. The key to this growth was Candler's ingenious marketing strategies which included having the company's employees and sales representatives distribute complimentary coupons for Coca-Cola.

Coupons were mailed to potential customers and were also placed in selected magazines. As an enticement to and support for stores to participate, The Company gave them free syrup to cover the costs of the free drinks. It is estimated that between 1894 and 1913 one in nine Americans had received a free Coca-Cola, for a total of 8,500,000 free drinks. By 1895,

Candler announced to shareholders that Coca-Cola was served in every state in United States.

Coupons first saw widespread use in the United States in 1909, when C.W. Post used coupons to help sell breakfast cereals and other products. Today, more than 2,800 consumer packaged goods companies offer coupons for discounts and products. In 2011, U.S. consumers used coupons to save 4.6 billion dollars on their purchases of consumer packaged goods.

PRINTABLE COUPON USAGE STATISTICS

According to NCH Marketing Services' 49th annual review of the U.S. coupon distribution, Consumer Packaged Goods Manufacturers distributed 315 billion coupons in 2013. Also, in 2013, consumers redeemed 2.8 billion coupons with a corresponding face-value redeemed cost savings of $200 million for Consumer Packaged Manufacturers.

According to recent research from the Promotion Marketing Association's (PMA) Coupon Council, many consumers are already taking advantage of the savings opportunities. The recent PMA Coupon Council Internet Survey of 1,000 people found that:

• 89 percent of the overall population reported that they use coupons when shopping (for grocery, household and healthcare items at supermarkets).

•97 percent of primary shoppers report that they use coupons at supermarkets.

•Coupon users report an average of 7% savings on their grocery bill with coupons.

"Consumers love coupons—they are a great way to economize, stretch the grocery bill and try new products for less than retail price," says Charles Brown, co-chair of the PMA Coupon Council. Particularly when shoppers are pinched by rising gas and energy costs, as well as increasing food prices, coupons offer an easy chance to save. All consumers have to do is organize their shopping to buy items with the coupons available to them—whether in their newspaper, in their mailbox, in the store, or on the internet, Brown added.

Typical Savings Studies have shown that shoppers who spend 20 minutes per week clipping and organizing their coupons can save up to $1,000 per year. (with an average annual family grocery bill of $5,000, that means 20 minutes could result in a 20% savings from coupons). The typical family saves between $5.20 and $9.60 per week using coupons. (46% of shoppers) still achieve an average $7.00 weekly savings on their grocery bill.

PMA Coupon Council co-chair Matthew Tilley adds, "in this environment, shoppers can be particularly responsive to coupon offers. But so far in 2008, CPG Marketers haven't really changed the number of coupons available, therefore, consumer redemption is steady with last year. That's a significant change because until last year, we saw 15 years of declining coupon redemption in the U.S."

DIGITAL COUPON STATISTICS

The digital coupon audience is growing faster than expected, says eMarketer. This year, more than half of US adult internet users, or 102.5 million people will redeem a digital coupon via any device for either online or offline shopping. eMarketer adds, "mobile has played a significant part in digital couponing in 2013 – more than 28% of people who own a mobile device redeemed a coupon this year. Nearly 70% of mobile coupon users will access coupons via smartphone. "We expect 42.1 million people to use a coupon obtained via app, mobile internet, or mobile barcode this year," says eMarketer.

CHAPTER TWO
WHAT IS A COUPON?

According to Webster's Dictionary, a coupon is a printed form, often distributed as part of an advertisement, entitling the bearer to purchase a specific item of merchandise at a discount, or, a similar form which may be substituted to the issuer to obtain goods or information.

According to Word Net Dictionary, a coupon is a negotiable certificate that can be detached and redeemed as needed, like a voucher.

Lastly, according to the Merriam Webster's Dictionary, a coupon is a certificate or similar evidence of a purchase redeemable in premiums.

As great as these definitions appear to be, I know that a coupon is a great method whereby we save money. More importantly, and this is what I would like for you to <u>always</u> remember, a coupon is FREE MONEY!!!

CHAPTER THREE
THE PROCESS OF A SUPERMARKET COUPON

If you have ever used coupons at the grocery store, then you know the routine. You cut coupons out, take them to the store and use them to get discounts on certain products. Once the cashier accepts the coupon, the store has a problem. It now has a small scrap of paper that is worth cash, but in order to get the cash the store has to mail the coupon to the manufacturer.

On the back of most coupons in fine print, the manufacturer lists the mailing address and states that it will also reimburse the store some amount of money for processing – typically 8 cents per coupon.

Redeeming a coupon would not be that bad if there were only a few of them, but major grocery and retail chains collect millions of them. The whole process seems hopelessly antiquated, but coupons remain enormously popular and that is why they continue. A coupon is, essentially, FREE MONEY, and FREE MONEY is hard to stop.

Once you hand the cashier your coupon(s), the cashier scans them and puts them into the cash drawer or some other designated place. What happens next depends on the store, but here's a typical process.

At the end of the day the coupons in each cash drawer are added as if they were cash. That amount is added to the cash sum to be sure the overall total for the drawer is accurate. Then all of the manufacturers' coupons (and any coupons issued by the grocer), are sent in plastic bags or pouches to the store's corporate headquarters, typically once a week.

In big store chains, the value of the coupons can easily total several million dollars per week. There is a person in headquarters who is in charge of processing the coupons. That person boxes all of the bags of coupons, (still separated by the individual stores from which they have come), and ships them to a third party Clearinghouse. This is where the real work starts. The Clearinghouse has to sort through millions of coupons, largely by hand. The first goal is to separate the coupons by manufacturer. Another goal is to separate coupons with scan able UPC codes from damaged (torn, smudged, etc.) coupons. This is so much hand work that some Clearinghouses pay other Clearinghouses – in Mexico, for example, to do part of the work.

One system places the coupons, that can be scanned, face up on a conveyor belt, where they are advanced under a scanner that reads the UPC codes and tallies the amounts. The system then adds up the total value of each manufacturer's coupon. Damaged coupons that cannot be scanned have to be sorted by hand and added up separately.

The other system is to do the whole thing by hand.

The Clearinghouse then sends all the sorted coupons with an invoice to the manufacturer. Several things can happen there.

The manufacturer might reimburse the Clearinghouse for the amount of the invoice. If so, then, the Clearinghouse will send a check to the store for the amount of the coupons, or the manufacturer will send a check directly to the store, plus shipping and handling. The whole cycle takes about a month.

In many cases, the manufacturer will recount the coupons to avoid fraud – a process that may send the coupons through another Clearinghouse!

BARCODES

Most grocery store coupons have a set of numbers (12) under each coupon called the Barcode or UPC (Universal Product Code). In fact, nearly every item that you purchase from a grocery store, department store and mass merchandiser, has a UPC bar code on it somewhere.

Whether you realized it or not, these numbers mean a lot. If the very first number is a five (5), this tells the computer to double that coupon (if the store offers it). If it starts with any other number, usually the coupon value is not doubled. For example, if the very first number is a nine (9), then the computer will not double the coupon value.

The next five (5) numbers are the Manufacturer's Identification Number, which should be the same on the product that you are purchasing. The next three (3) numbers refer to the product code. The next two (2) numbers refer to the value of the coupon. This indicates how a particular item will be discounted.

The last number is the check digit. This digit lets the scanner determine if it scanned the number correctly or not. A person employed by the manufacturer, called the UPC Coordinator, is responsible for assigning item numbers to products, making sure the same code is not used on more than one product and retiring codes as products are removed from the product line, etc.

Now that you understand all of this, if a coupon does not scan, be patient, or perhaps call for the manager to assist you. Remember, because the UPC Coordinator assigns the numbers to millions of products, it is easy to make unintentional mistakes. Chill. Be patient. Your savings will be worth the wait!

CHAPTER FOUR
TWELVE REASONS TO SAVE MONEY
USING COUPONS

Before we discuss the reasons to save money, let me suggest this: Set a goal. It can be a 2, 4, or 6 month goal. Then get a large jar, basket, bucket, etc. During this time, as you grow in your couponing skills, put all of the money you are saving, each time you use a coupon, into the suggested device. At the end of your goal, count your savings, and do one of the suggested ideas...GO FOR IT!!!

◆ **VACATION:** a vacation is always nice even if it is only for a night or weekend.

◆ **PURCHASE FURNITURE:** perhaps you would like to have another or a particular piece of furniture to complete a room.

◆ **COLLEGE EDUCATION:** perhaps this could be a long term goal.

◆ **DOWN PAYMENT ON SOMETHING SPECIAL –** just for you.

◆ **A LONG TERM GOAL –** you decide for what.

◆ **A SHORT TERM GOAL** – easily obtainable.

◆ **REMODEL HOUSE:** add on/change something.

◆ **CLOTHING (FUR COAT):**...yes, sure looks good on you.

◆ **CRUISE:** this would be a lovely treat.

◆ **START A SAVINGS ACCOUNT:** or add to the one you already have (increase).

◆ **IT'S A GOOD THING TO DO** – sure is.

◆ **PROVE TO YOUSELF AND OTHERS...I CAN DO THIS**

CHAPTER FIVE
COUPON PROVERBS

I wrote the following and thought I would call them Coupon Proverbs. They are short sayings from all of the chapters of this book.

~Read the words, not the pictures on coupons.

~Look for stores that "double" coupons. The value of your savings are better.

~Before you go shopping, arrange all of your coupons. This saves much time.

~Join rebate clubs online.

~Set aside one-hour per day for couponing.

~Remember that couponing is a means by which to save money.

~Have fun.

~Stacking is a term that means to use a manufacturer's coupon and a store's coupon together for greater savings.

~Ask the store cashier or sales representative if the store is offering any money-saving coupons every time you shop.

~Don't overlook any coupon source.

~Remember to use the store discount card at the end of the transaction and "watch the savings on the register go down."

~Get rain checks for items that are out stock at the time of shopping.

~Shop the clearance/reduced item section of the store and use your coupons together with the items that are already discounted.

~Small help you to save big. Do not despise the 25 cent coupons...they add up.

~Couponing is not just a hobby, but it's a money saving strategy game.

~Ask out-of-town family members to send you their unused coupons.

~The "best" time to print internet coupons is at the beginning of the month.

~Get an email account to use exclusively for couponing.

~A sale is not always a bargain.

~Always shop prepared and organized.

~Do not grocery shop when you are hungry.

CHAPTER SIX
COUPON TERMS (FULL LISTING)

Blinkies – In store, (smart source coupon), that is dispensed near the product, usually in a red blinking box.

BOGO or B1G1 - Buy one get one free.

BRU - Babies-R-Us.

Catalina – A coupon that is dispensed at the register after purchase.

C/O - Cents off coupon.

Codes - Refunds that require only a UPC number that is written on a cash register tape.

Coufund - For coupons that need some proof of purchase such as UPC's attached.

Cpns- Manufacturer's coupons.

CRT - Cash register tape.

DCRT- Dated cash register tape.

DCRTC - Dated cash register tape with the price circled.

DND - Do Not Double (the coupon is not supposed to be doubled).

Double coupon- A coupon that a grocery store doubles in value. Usually it is up to $1.00.

FL - Food Lion (or Florida).

Free Item Coupon - A coupon that allows you to get the product completely free.

FSI - Free Standing Inserts. These are the actual terms for the coupons you get in your Sunday newspaper. Also referred to as Sunday Supplement Coupons or Insert Coupons.

HBA - The Health and Beauty Aid section in the grocery store.

HDA - Hot Deal Alert or Home Delivered Ad.

HT or HgT- Hang tags for refunds or coupons that are hanging on a product.

HT - Harris Teeter.

HTH - Hope this helps.

ISO - In search of.

LTD – Limited. As on a refund form, it will say you are limited to a certain number of purchases.

MFG – Manufacturer.

MFR – Manufacturer.

Money + - Premiums that require money in addition to a proof of purchase.

NAZ - Name, address, zip code.

NB - National Brand.

NBQ - National Brand Qualifier.

NED - No expiration date.

Nfp - Refund form found in a newspaper.

NT WT - Net weight.

OAS – A coupon that is good on one purchase, of any size.

OP - Original post.

OSI - On a single item.

OYNSO - On Your Next Shopping Order.

POP - Proof of purchase.

PP - Purchase price.

PPHF - Paypal handling fee.

Q or Qualifier- The Proof of Purchase, required for a refund offer that is physically taken from that package.

RAOK - Random act of kindness.

SASE - Self Addressed Stamped Envelope.

SF - Store form.

SMP - Specially marked packages.

SS - Sunday Supplement Coupons (FSI).

Super doubles – Coupons that are doubled $1 + in value (ie, a $1 coupon = $2, etc)

SWEEPS - Sweepstakes form.

Tear pad - A pad of refund forms that is found hanging from a store shelf or display.

TMF - Try Me Free.

Triple Coupon – A coupon that a grocery store triples in value.

TRU - Toys-R-Us.

UPC - Universal Product Code.

WD - Winn Dixie.

WSL - While supplies last.

YMMV - Your Mileage May Vary.

CHAPTER 7
COUPON EXCUSES

1) YOU HAVE TO BUY A NEWSPAPER: for the price of a newspaper, the paper pays for itself. The moment you buy the paper, you are on your way to making and saving money.

2) CLIPPING COUPONS TAKES TIME: couponing takes time that is well spent. With the proper time management, it doesn't take as much time as you might think. It is, however, time that is spent wisely.

3) GETTING A NEWSPAPER INVITES LOTS OF ADDITIONAL ADVERTISING INTO YOUR HOME: not necessarily. With the proper discipline and focus, you do not have to sponsor the other advertisements. Know what you need and toss the rest.

4) MANY OF THE COUPONS WILL BE FOR THINGS YOU NEITHER NEED OR WANT: knowing where to search for the things you specifically need will eliminate this from happening. Also, if you don't need a particular coupon consider sharing it with someone else or send it to the military. Someone else may be able to benefit.

5) THE SAME COUPONS TEND TO BE OFFERED OVER AND OVER AGAIN: this is a good thing especially if it's an item that you frequently use. If you didn't use it last month, perhaps you can use it this month.

6) SHOPPING WITH COUPONS TAKES LONGER: if you have to hunt up and down the aisle in search of the item you have a coupon for, then probably yes, but if you know your store as a frequent shopper you should not have this problem. With the proper preparation and

time management, shopping with coupons will become a breeze.

7) THE BOTTOM LINE: perhaps the most dedicated coupon clippers can overcome these minor hurdles and still achieve overall savings. Once you begin couponing, you will find it very difficult to buy something without a coupon. Yes, couponing may initially have its challenges, like anything else that is new, however, once you get used to cutting your grocery bill by 40-50%, you will not want to pay full price again.

CHAPTER 8
DIFFERENT TYPES OF COUPONS

•<u>Restaurant</u> – Google: (web browser) <u>printable</u> <u>restaurant</u> <u>coupons</u> for a list of restaurant coupons. You will get a list of restaurants that are available for coupons. The best site for this is <u>www.BeFrugal.com</u>. Next, select and click "restaurant."   Then click "printable". You will find over 250 printable restaurant coupons that are available to be printed and used.

•<u>Manufacturer</u> - Manufacturer's coupons are a specific type of discount coupon that can be used towards the purchase of specific products made by a given company.

•<u>Store</u> – This refers to a coupon that is offered in the store.

•<u>Catalina</u> – This coupon is also known as a check-out coupon.   It is printed in the store, along with your receipt from the store. For errors with the printing of the coupon, contact them directly at 1-888-8coupon.

•<u>Blinkie</u> – "Blinkies" are coupons that are distributed in stores by a SmartSource Coupon Machine. The nickname "blinkie" refers to the dispensing machines with a blinking light that is designed to attract your attention as you walk down the aisle. These "blinkie machines are typically found directly in front of the product being offered at discount. While walking down the aisles, these "blinkie" machines are typically located directly in front of the merchandise.

•<u>Coupon Hang Tag</u> – These coupons, unlike those that are coupons on their own or the peelies that stick to products, hang around the neck or body of a product. They are usually pretty small and just look like extra product information, but they are coupons in disguise! And, they can really help you create great savings sometimes! Also, coupon hang tags are almost always manufacturer coupons, so you can still pair them with a store coupon (stacking), and save even more money!

•<u>Peelies</u> – They are found directly on the product. "Peelies" generally are the coupons that are attached directly to the product and must be peeled off. Generally they indicate "use me now". These coupons are frequently unnoticed at the time of purchase, but generally can be removed and redeemed at any time before the expiration date. Occasionally, peelies are printed with a disclaimer that indicates, they are only valid when removed by the cashier, at the time of purchase.

•<u>Internet</u> – These coupons are found on the internet. They can be printed at home and used at any store. They are usually called printable internet coupons.

•<u>Tear pad</u> – Appearing somewhat like little notepads, tear pads are pads of coupons that are often stocked on the shelf or product display. They are sometimes easily located and offered on cardboard in-aisle displays.

Customers may simply tear a coupon off of the pad and use any time before the expiration date. Tear pad coupons are generally redeemable at any store that accepts manufacturer coupons; however, store chains may print tear pads for use only at their chain of stores. In this case, the coupon should indicate REDEEMABLE ONLY AT xxx store and will usually have the logo of the store chain printed on the coupon.

•<u>Facebook</u> – To get coupons on facebook (and there are many), you must have a facebook account. In the "search box," type "facebook coupon list."

•<u>ECoupons</u> – also called Electronic Coupons, are manufacturers' paperless coupons that are loaded onto your grocery card before you shop. ECoupons can be the easiest coupons to use because you don't have to clip, organize, file, store, or lug anything into the store. In order to use ECoupons, you must register online and provide your customer account information and loyalty card numbers for each store that you want to register.

Once registered, you will be able to browse and select the ECoupons that you want. Everything is stored and tracked by your loyalty card and once you register all your grocery cards with the Ecoupon websites, you just load the coupons to your card, scan your card, and collect your savings. When you go to check out at the store, you will swipe your customer card and the ECoupons will automatically be deducted from your purchase when you buy the qualifying items.

With using ECoupons, you may, however, experience technical failure, which sometimes can be an issue. For example, if an ECoupon fails to get deducted during checkout, the customer has no proof to show the cashier the value of the coupon. Additionally, ECoupons cannot be stacked with other coupons, unlike paper coupons. Also, ECoupons are not doubled. You only get the face value of the coupon.

Some Top ECoupon Sites:

A. **Cellfire** is an electronic coupon service that has partnered with select grocery stores customer loyalty programs. This service will allow you to load ECoupons from your computer onto your grocery store customer loyalty card. This offer, however, is only available at a select number of stores. For more information go to cellfire.com and register.

B. **Shortcuts** are paperless electronic coupons that are loaded to customer's loyalty card at select grocery stores and drugstores. For more information go to shortcuts.com and register.

C. **Zavers** is an electronic coupon service that handles ECoupons for select grocery stores. To register, go to Zavers.com.

D. **Saving Star** is a grocery ECoupon service that allows you to save paperless coupons to your supermarket and drugstore loyalty cards. However, unlike most paper coupons, when Saving Star ECoupons are redeemed at the store, the amount does not immediately come off your grocery total. Instead, the amount of the redeemed coupons is accumulated in your Saving Star account. When the amount reaches $5.00, you can opt to be paid through Pay Pal, or with an Amazon gift card. Or, you may donate the saved amount, to a non-profit organization of

E. your choice. For more information, visit Saving Star.com.

F. **Upromise** is a simple, yet powerful idea. Savings through this program and your everyday spending with Upromise partners, will allow you to create a college savings account. The money you earn from your everyday spending with select Upromise partners, goes directly into your Upromise account. For more information, visit Upromise.com.

G. The three main companies, in this area, that offer coupons in selected newspapers each week are:

1) Smartsource (SS)

2) Redplum (RP)

3) Procter & Gamble (P&G)

CHAPTER 9
GOOD STUFF TO KNOW
ABOUT COUPONING

•The number one thing you must do before you start couponing is: create an email account to be used exclusively for coupon-related information, correspondence, offers and promotions. With this special email account, you will be happy to open your account because it will only be something relating to coupons and saving money.

•Also, by using this email account, you will be prepared and properly organized in customizing all coupon-related savings.

•Many sites require that you register with that site before you are able to print any coupons. Go ahead and register with them using your special email account. You will be surprised at the number of companies who will email you coupons on a daily basis.

•Please, from this moment on...think of coupons as FREE MONEY!

•To be the best at couponing and to save lots of money, there are four key elements needed on the roads to success! They are time, patience, genuine interest, and organization. Of the four, organization is the "bulls-eye" motivation to saving money. If you are not organized, you will become impatient and quit. Don't do it (stick with it)...saving money is fun!!!

•Couponing is a business!!! Why? Because the company makes money off of every item that is purchased and you save money off of every item that is purchased – only if you use the coupon and not leave them in the car (smile).

•Remember that initially the more time you invest in getting set up – the better you will become at couponing. Initially, you may only save $15-$20, but don't become discouraged. The $100.00 is on the way!!! STAY FOCUSED...STAY ORGANIZED.

•Coupons are the same as cash money – free money.

•Stores usually receive .08 cents per coupon.

•It is illegal to copy or reprint coupons. Fraudulent coupons are illegal! Also, please do not knowingly use coupons after the expiration date, unless the store accepts expired coupons.

•If you have any expired coupons, you may send them to the Military Troops and their families at www.OCPNET.org. They are allowed to use expired coupons up to six months only at overseas locations.

•Most internet websites will only allow you to print coupons twice.

•Using coupons puts money back into the pockets of grocery stores. We are not taking advantage of the stores. They are doing just fine (profits are up). According to the CIC (Coupon Information Center), only about 10% of Americans shop with coupons on a regular basis. The other 90% of Americans pay through the roof for groceries. Therefore, please do not feel

guilty about using coupons. The stores continue to make money and we will continue to save! Also, remember that coupons generates repeat business and encourage customers to return again and again.

•Learn and know your store's policy on couponing. For example, do they offer double coupons? Do they have a limit concerning the number of coupons you may use per transaction? Do they accept "all" types of coupons (internet, manufacturer, catalina, etc.).

•The best deals offered are stacking (manufacturer & store coupon together) ...go for it!

•Paper coupons offer more flexibility to Couponers, which in the long run, will save them more money.

•My policy is: Use your store's customer card at the end of a transaction. Watch the savings go down! Additionally, give the cashier your coupons after you use your store savings card. THERE IS NO SPECIAL REASON FOR THIS, IT'S MENTAL. I CAN CALCULATE BETTER IF I SEE IT. This is a personal preference. You may adopt this shopping practice.

•In order to maximize your savings, the "best" printable internet coupons can be found at the beginning of the month. The coupons that are released earlier in the month are plentiful.

•Most manufacturers set a limit as far as how many coupons they will allow each customer to print, for a particular product. After that number is reached, they

yank the coupon. Your personal print limit is almost always two per coupon, per month. It re-sets at the beginning of the next month.

•Generally, manufacturers will ask you to enter your email address before you can print the coupons.

•Clipping coupons is worth the effort to save money in your family. Unless you are a millionaire, every little bit helps.

•If at all possible, wait to shop on Wednesday after you receive the local grocery store flyer (ad), and when products, especially meats, are freshest.

•Try not to worry or become impatient if it takes a little bit more time at the register while using coupons. It adds up quickly! As a courtesy, let the person behind you in line know that you have coupons to use. They will appreciate you for this!

•Ask out of town family to send you their coupons.

•Pay attention to your coupons.

•Subscribe to more than one newspaper (Sunday) to get coupons. Try some out-of-town newspapers. They have coupons, too.

•If you are using EBT (food stamps), and coupons, in Virginia, you will be charged tax on the coupons at the

end of your transaction.

•99% of coupons used are physical coupons rather than Smartphone or IPhone users using a code to get a discount, deal, or coupon.

•Whenever you are planning to go retail shopping, always check the internet. There may be a coupon for that particular store. There are many retail stores that offer printable internet coupons. Always look for a sale before you go shopping.

•If you seriously want to save lots of money, you need to be on the lookout for every opportunity you can find to save money.

•You should not pay full price for anything. The discounts are out there!

•Once you start using coupons and saving money, you will not know why you ever paid full price for anything. You won't want to anymore. You will be proud to share your new knowledge of coupons with everyone.

•Impulse buying is a no-no. Proper planning and preparation are always good.

• Be polite when you are using coupons.

• Distractions: distractions are a "no-no" when grocery shopping and using coupons. It is a "good" idea when trying to master the balancing act of shopping with coupons, to try shopping with as few distractions as possible (family, kids, husband, impatient people, anxious people, etc.) For a while, this might include shopping alone or when the kids are in school, late night shopping, etc. I strongly recommend, until you get the "hang of couponing," that you shop when you are best able to concentrate on what you are doing. This is serious business! (smile)

• Trial and error: all couponers, and you will too, have their favorite couponing system. None of us shop the exact same way. There is, however, no right or wrong way to get set to go shopping with coupons, except not to do it at all. There are shortcuts mentioned in this book, and by trying some of them, you might find using coupons a lot less frustrating than you thought.

• Take notes: there are times when you might want to make a note to remind yourself of a particular savings as you shop. This becomes especially helpful when sale items are spreaded around the store. Notes are important when items at the register does not ring up properly. By having good notes, you are readily able to save everyone some time and energy when checking out.

•If you plan to go to more than one store, make a list for each store and separate coupons accordingly.

•When using the customer rewards card, make certain that you have the card readily available or in an easy place to find. If not, it will be one last thing to fumble around to find, once you are at the check-out counter.

•Coupons are an "easy" way to save money.

•Couponing is not just a hobby, but, it is a money strategy game.

•Be flexible about brands. Name brands do not always save you money.

•Get ready to save before you go shopping. This eliminates wasted time in the store.

•Every sale is not a bargain.

•In the beginning, take small baby steps so you won't become overwhelmed with using coupons.

CHAPTER 10
HOW TO APPROACH COUPONING

•Take it slow!

•Always look for sale before you shop

•If you seriously want to save lots of money couponing, you need to be on the lookout for every opportunity you can find to save money.

•You should not pay full price for anything from this point on. The savings and discounts are out there.

•Impulse buying is a no-no. Planning and preparation are key goals.

•One step at a time.

•Start slow and stay organized. It will take some time to develop a workable system for you–hang in there.

•Do not try to do it all at once. You will become discouraged and frustrated and not succeed at all.

•Take baby steps, listen and learn as you go. This way, you will easily save money every single time you step foot into the store. Tackle one store at a time and one type of coupon at a time.

•Once you learn the basics, you will be able to apply them anywhere.

•Couponing is a lot of fun!!

•Approach couponing with a positive attitude.

•Stick with couponing...give it a fair try...go for it...do not give up!

CHAPTER 11
17 COUPON TIPS©

♦Double your savings by using a store coupon with a manufacturer savings coupon. This process is called stacking.

♦Ask the stores sales representative or the cashier for any money saving coupons or savings that you might use towards your purchase.

♦When an item is 10/$10.00, remember you do not have to buy all ten items. If you buy one item, the price will be $1.00 each. Ask if the store will allow you to mix and match products. This is especially true with Food Lion stores; however, for clarification ask the store manager or cashier if this is their store's policy before shopping.

♦When finding "buy one get one item free specials," ask the store manager if you purchase only one item, if that item will be half-priced.

♦Read the coupon words not the pictures on the coupon. Sometimes the picture will show a larger size product, when actually it is worded "on any size item."

♦To help prevent impulse buying, jot down a shopping list and stick to it.

♦When making a shopping list, if you have a coupon for a particular item, write the letter "c" beside the item or tracking.   This helps you to stay organized when using your coupons.

♦Try using the coupon when the item is on sale. This will give you a better deal and much more savings.

♦Do not overlook any coupon source.

♦Compare prices from store-to-store. It is very helpful to use the store's advertisement. You will get the best deals this way.

♦Spending just a few extra minutes online before going to the grocery store will save you lots of money.

♦If you are planning to be an avid coupon shopper, you might want to purchase a large binder to organize your coupons.

♦Familiarize yourself with your favorite store's coupon policy:

>　*Does the store double coupons?

>　*Does the store accept internet coupons?

>　*Is there a limit on the number of items that can be purchased if coupons are used?

♦Use the store discount card at the end of the transaction. It does the "eyes" good to see the savings.

♦Always think of coupons as "free" money.

◆Get rain checks for items that are advertised as sales items if the store is out of that particular item. At most stores, rain checks do not expire.

◆Have fun and save lots of money using coupons.

CHAPTER 12
21 MONEY SAVING COUPON IDEAS©

*Register   with all stores for a customer discount or rewards card. Scan the card after all purchases have been rung up in order to "watch" the savings and prices decrease.

*Look for in-store coupons – example – Food Lion, Safeway, Kroger, CVS, Walgreens, Rite Aid, Target, Dollar General, Family Dollar, etc.

*Look for stores that offer double couple days. If you are not sure, ask the customer service desk about the store's coupon policy when you get to the store.

*Get rain checks.   Most of them never expire. This allows you to still get the sale price of an item at a later date.

*When you are dissatisfied with an item, let the manufacturer know directly.

*Before you go department retail store shopping, Google the store to see if there's a coupon available to use at that store. Also, once arriving at the store, don't be afraid to ask the cashier if he/she has any money-saving coupons. (example – Old Navy Coupons)

*Avon is a product that is cheaper to order on line. Additionally, shipping and handling charges may be free.

*Shop in the "clearance" section of the store. You will find great bargain prices on many items.

*Purchase an Entertainment Book that may be loaded with many local coupons and savings for dining, travel, hotels, car rental, etc. The book pays for itself!! It is published annually and usually can be purchased at drugstores like Walgreens.

*Register with stores, restaurants, etc., to receive special savings and holiday event specials. For example, sign up with Old Navy and be the first to know about in store sales or promotions.

*Contact the customer service department for every business and ask if the store has any money-saving coupons. For example, every product has a distributor and manufacturer. If you do not know who the manufacturer is, then look on the package and find out. Once you have that information, Google the name and you will be led to the manufacturer's website. Once on the manufacturer's website, look for the "contact us" tab. You will then receive the email and/or physical mailing address. This is when you need to give the manufacturer any positive feedback concerning the products they offer and you can also ask for money-saving coupons to use towards your next purchase. When writing them, be honest and positive.

*Look for coupon swap boxes when shopping.

*Look in the circulars of the Sunday's newspapers like – Progress Index, Richmond Times Dispatch, Washington Post, New York Times, etc. Each week you will find many great money-saving coupons.

*When shopping, do not be afraid to ask the cashier/customer service manager of a particular store, if the store has any money saving coupons that you might use. Many distributors leave coupons with the store manager for distribution to customers.

*Join a wholesale savings club such as Sam's Club, Costco or others. They offer opportunities for you to save money, especially on bulk size items.

*Swap coupons with other people. Also, do not hesitant to ask neighbors, friends, out of town family members, if you can have their coupons from the Sunday newspaper. The more, the merrier!

*Register with restaurants that offer "free" meals on your birthday. For example Red Lobster, Quiznos, etc. Also, throughout the year, they will email you special coupons.

*Enter sweepstakes – you might win!!!

*Be flexible about brands. Buy the items for which you have coupons/discounts for. Name brands do not always save you money.

*Join rebate programs with drugstores such as: CVS, Walgreens, Rite Aid and others.

*Watch for special savings at drugstores. They have begun to offer great prices on items we use the most.

CHAPTER 13
TIME MANAGEMENT

• There are many people who say couponing is not worth the money you save because it takes so much time. Yes, using coupons can take a lot of time; however, it does not have to. The amount of time it takes is really up to you. If you stay organized, have patience, and remain focused, you will enjoy couponing, and save lots of money.

• Limit Deal Finding Time. Your time is valuable. Do not spend it all on the internet looking for coupons. There are lots and lots of frugal internet websites, but you do not need to go to all of them because many of them repeat the same deals. The best practice is to pick 3-4 good sites and stick with them. They will have a lot to offer.

• Do not spend a lot of time driving all over town. You probably only need to shop at 1-2 grocery stores and 1-2 drugstores. Most stores offer the same deals – just at different times. Learn your stores' sales cycles and you will have a better understanding of what I mean. There may be sales items at a store across town. If you have time, go for it, otherwise try not to wear yourself out trying to save .50 cent (smile)

• Get ready "before" you go shopping. If you have everything ready when you hit the stores, you will spend a lot less time shopping. You will need to take with you the coupons, the grocery list, the sales ad, and your coupon book. A good practice and a time management skill is to write, a "c" beside the item you have coupons for and how many of that item you plan to buy. This will save you a few extra minutes in the store. Stay focused!!! Do not become sidetracked or distracted by "this is the best sale ever."

• Every sale is advertised as "the best sale ever."

• Buy only what your family uses!

• Decrease time at the store. Now, that your list is ready and even tells how many items you need of a particular item, you do not necessarily have to pull the coupon from your book until you get to the aisle where the item is. Although, this is my practice...it is not the only way. Perhaps you may have a better way to conceptualize your time at the store.

• A good practice is to always have your coupon book with you. Do not leave home without it! You never know when you will unexpectedly use your book. It is better to have it and not need it, than to need it and not have it! Additionally, this will substitute for the mistake of missing unforeseen savings opportunities. Remember, to master the art of savings, we must favorably benefit by every means available.

CHAPTER 14
HOW TO ORGANIZE A USER-FRIENDLY COUPON BOOK

Organizing a user-friendly coupon book is a piece of cake – at least that is what I think (smile).

Get a coupon book that is comfortable and convenient for "you" to use. I use a three ring binder type coupon book because I am a serious coupon-minded individual and my collection of coupons requires this type of binder. Note: I did not start out with this size book, but found over time that is was the best and most comfortable for me and my shopping habits.

Perhaps you are just getting started; therefore, you might begin with a much smaller size book until your coupons begin to accumulate.

I have recommended several coupon categories that should be considered as you begin to organize, select your book and begin to collect and use your coupons efficiently. As a matter of fact, my book has the exact same categories listed below. Whatever categories you select, you might find that alphabetizing the categories will help with your organization. This process is easier, less complicated and saves lots of time when you have to look for a coupon. All of the categories should be self-explanatory except the miscellaneous products. I use this category when I don't know where to put a coupon. You will see the categories, drugstores, shopping stores, and rain checks at the end of the list because of their category – not food items.

Also, with the shopping stores category, you might want to sub-categorize this according to your favorite retail stores to shop. The same concept can be used for drugstores.

Perhaps you may want to add to this list, but please do not have so many categories that you become confused and can't remember. Plus, your coupon book will look junkie. Have fun with this!

COUPON CATEGORIES

AUTOMOTIVE

BABY PRODUCTS

BAKERY & BREAD

BAKING & SPICES

BEAUTY & PERSONAL HYGIENE

BEVERAGES

CANNED GOODS

CLEANING PRODUCTS

DAIRY

DESSERTS

ENTERTAINMENT & TRAVEL

FROZEN FOODS

MEAT

MISCELLANEOUS PRODUCTS

PASTA & READY MADE MEALS

PET FOOD & CARE

PRODUCE & VEGGIES

SNACKS

DRUGSTORES

SHOPPING STORES

RAINCHECKS

HOW TO ORGANIZE COUPONS

Now that you have nicely typed your categories on labels, let's move on. You are ready to organize your coupons for insertion.

I have found the best way to organize coupons is to place them in piles according to the categories you have just made. For example: group all of your baby products together, canned goods together, cleaning products together, snacks together, etc., **BEFORE YOU PUT THEM INTO YOUR BOOK**. This will keep you from having to flip back and forth so often.

After you have grouped all of the categories of coupons together, place the coupons behind its proper category in your book. Easy, right? Well, you have just completed your first coupon book. Congratulations!!!!!

CHAPTER 15
"FREE" STUFF WEBSITES

NOTE: every website has a "free stuff" tab. Don't be shy. Get some "stuff" free. These are the recommended sites that I use daily.

www.getitfree.us.com

www.coolsavings.com

www.freebiesfrenzy.com

www.freebizmag.com

www.slickdeal.net

www.freeflys.com

www.thatfreebiesite.com (best)

www.freebies.about.com (best)

www.thediscountconnection.com (best)

www.thefreesite.com

www.all-4-free.com

www.yesall4free.com

www.totallyfreecrap.com

www.sweetfreestuff.com

www.freestuff.com

www.thebucklist.blogspot.com

www.ilovefreethings.com

www.freestuffinder.com

www.thetop20sites.com

www.justfreestuff.com

www.heyitsfree.net

www.coolfreebielinks.com

www.get-free-coupons.com

www.freecoupons.com

www.free-n-cool.com

www.freestufftimes.com

www.twinsandtriplets.com

www.getfreebabycoupons.com

CHAPTER 16
"FREE" INTERNET COUPON WEBSITES
TO FIND COUPONS

There are literally thousands of free websites where you can find coupons, however, we don't need thousands of websites to be able to save lots of money – only a select few! I have gone through hundreds of sites and what I am sharing with you are the sites that I currently use and am proud to say that "they" work for me.

While using these sites, I find the exact products that I need. Perhaps you will too. Some or most of these sites will require you to register before researching products/coupons – or at least I strongly recommend it. This is mainly the reason for the special email address we talked about earlier. After you register with the site, you will notice there are many tabs like: bargains, local deals, coupons, browse, etc. If you would like to use paper coupons, then for all of these sites you have to look for the coupons tab then click printable.

Printable coupons allow you to print the coupons you desire. Sometimes you may have to download a special printer bar before you will be able to print from that particular site, but you should only have to download it once. Moreover, if you would prefer to shop online then do NOT look for printable instead look for online codes. Once you find the online codes for a particular discount, then follow the directions accordingly.

SPECIAL NOTE: I would like to strongly suggest that before you begin to use the websites that I am sharing with you, that you register with all of "your" favorite everything (stores, restaurants, retail stores, etc.) You will be amazed at what they will have to offer you. Enjoy!!!!!

FREE COUPON WEBSITES

www.coupons.com
(use different zip codes)

www.mommysavesbig.com

www.retailmenot.com

www.grocerycouponnetwork.com

www.familycoupondaily.com

www.shopathome.com

www.bargainblessings.com

www.hotcouponworld.com

www.dealigg.com

www.freefly's.com

www.shortcuts.com

www.slickdeal.net

www.smartsource.com

www.redplum.com

www.procterandgamble.com

www.cellfire.com

www.bargainez.com

www.couponmom.com

www.printable coupons.com

www.moneysavingmom.com

www.allyou.com

www.42.bricks.com

www.shortcuts.com

www.buxr.com

www.savings.com

www.cacoupondiva.com

www.about.com

www.moneycrashers.com

www.thebudgetbandit.com

www.grocerysmarts.com

www.ppgazette.com

www.bradsdeals.com

www.save.com

www.oohey.com

iams.com

www.printablecoupon

www.dealnews.com

www.forthemommas.com

www.couponnetwork.com

www.survivingthestores.com

www.befrugal.com

www.bsavings.com

www.commissarydeals.com
(commissary coupons)

www.facebookcouponlist.com

www.retailmenot.com

www.freeshipping.com

www.couboncabin.com

www.dealighted.com

www.dealcatcher.com

www.wowcoupons.com

www.kidseatfree.com

www.printableautorelatedcoupons.com

www.printablebeveragecoupons.com

www.printablecouponsanddeals.com

www.buxr.com

www.printablehealthcare.com

www.printablepetcarecoupons.com

www.hotworldcoupon.com

www.simplifiedsavings.com

www.cuckooforcoupondeals.com

www.dealsplus.com

www.save.com

www.familydollar.com

www.printablecoupons2013.com

www.gotodaily.com

www.qponning.com

www.couponcaboodle.com

www.quickprintcoupons.com

www.grocerycouponnetwork.com

www.youandyourfamily.com

www.internetdrugcoupons.com

www.pgeveryday.com

www.grocerysmarts.com

www.grocerywiz.com

www.valpak.com

www.cleaningproductsworld.com

www.savingsadvice.com

www.couponnetwork.com

www.survivingthestores.com

www.befrugal.com

www.bsavings.com

www.freeshipping.org

www.gotodaily.com

www.fatwallet.com

www.couponcabin.com

www.dealighted.com

www.slickdeals.com

www.wowcoupons.com

www.kidseatfree.com (restaurants in your area that offers good deals for kids) www.freeprintablecouponsrestaurants.com (use restaurant coupons and save on eating out)

www.printableautorelatedcoupons.com

www.printablebeveragecoupons.com

www.iams.com (animal coupons)

www.printablebabycoupons.com

www.printablecouponsanddeals.com

www.buxr.com

www.bricks.com

www.coupondivas.com

www.printablehealthcarecoupons.com

www.printablepersonalcarecoupons.com

www.printablepetcarecoupons.com

www.wow-coupons.com

www.familydollar.com

www.dollargeneral.com

www.save.com

www.buxrhotdealscoupons.com

wwwhotcouponworld.com

www.printablecoupons2013.com

www.moneysavingmom.com

www.dealsplus.com

www.bargainblessings.com

www.parents.com

www.honest.com

www.walmart.com

www.mycoupons.com

www.simplifiedsavings.com

www.cuckooforcoupondeals.com

www.centsoff.com

www.wisebread.com

www.ableshoppers.com

www.bargainist.com

www.dealocker.com

www.dealsofAmerica.com

www.pricesandcoupons.com

www.pricey-net.com

www.mygrocerydeals.com

www.shopittome.com

COUPON SITES THAT REQUIRE NO REGISTRATION

www.freeprintable.com

www.coolfreebielinks.com

www.coupon-coupons.com

www.workingmom.com

www.gloster.com

www.suite101.com

www.mysavings.com

www.ezinemark.com

www.couponclinch.com

www.babycouponsfreeonline.com

www.momasaves.com

www.couponcabin.com

www.floppycats.com

CHAPTER 17
THE FUTURE OF COUPONS

The latest information on About.com reports that the future of coupons is filled with fast paced, techy-type platforms for distribution, unlike it's ancestral Sunday newspaper inserts. For some, learning how it all works is fascinating. For others, the only information they want is what button they need to push. Either way, advertising companies are betting on the future of cell phones and websites to put coupons into consumer's hands. Here is a glimpse into the future of coupons.

BROADBAND VIDEO

Broadband video has a strong potential as a powerful extension to television advertising. The TV-like video content can be seen on a website using a high-speed broadband connection. Currently there are two types of on-demand internet video – in-stream and in-banner.

IN-STREAM VIDEOS

In-stream videos, which appear on a website, are generally 15 to 30 seconds long and appear when a user click on specific content. The advertising is primarily syndicated video content, much like what you see on TV. Generally a banner, which may contain a coupon, is featured as support, alongside the video.

IN-BANNER VIDEO

In-banner video are videos embedded in or expanded from a banner on a website. Some of these videos do not begin until the user clicks on them, but some are designed to expand and run whether the user clicks or not. Once expanded, the in-banner ad can feature custom designs that often include a coupon.

MOBILE DEVICES

Mobile devices are quickly growing in popularity as a way to distribute coupons since they are in nearly everyone's hands, especially while out shopping or traveling. There are several ways to deliver coupons to a consumer's mobile device including utilizing short message services (SMS), wireless application protocol (WAP), sites and dynamic downloadable applications.

SHORT MESSAGE SERVICE (SMS)

SMS is available on nearly all of the newer cell phones in the market. Advertisers can design a coupon to be redeemed by the consumer by bringing the phone in-store or via a code that can be entered into a web if it's an online purchase.

WIRELESS APPLICATION PROTOCOL(WAP) SITES

WAP sites that are designed for the small screen size of mobile phones. WAP sites can be assessed by the user when they use their mobile internet browsers. Coupons can be put on the WAP sites, along with other information such as store finders, hours of store operation, directions, etc.

MOBILE APPLICATIONS

Mobile phone users can now download a software application or program, typically from a website or wapsite to view, use and save coupons. These software applications are saved to the device deck on the phone and when selected by the user and feature mobile coupons from participating advertisers.

COUPON BOOK FEES

What an exciting time for you as you begin to save money using coupons. Here is another exciting deal that will help you reach your goals.

If you do not have the time, let me assist you. You may contact me at <u>kupongirl50@yahoo.com</u> for information regarding coupon services offered to help you save money.

In summary, for a one time book fee, based on the size of the coupon book you wish to maintain, I will provide the services most needed by you. I will even maintain your book on a weekly basis for a monthly fee.

Again, it is my pleasure to help you begin or continue this couponing experience that I really enjoy. Join me in saving money as we shop.

Best wishes,

Sharon Johnson

ABOUT THE AUTHOR

Sharon has had many wonderful and fascinating jobs throughout the State of Virginia. To name a few, Television and Radio Stations, Public Library in her hometown, Virginia Attorney General's Office, Congressman's Office, Probation Officer, School Teacher, Cashier, and some others, all of which she adores. Sharon, however, says that besides raising a wonderful son, she thoroughly enjoys couponing equally well. She has been an avid couponer for several years and has had the opportunity to become very familiar with the "art" of couponing. Sharon teaches coupon workshops in her hometown and abroad and is very enthusiastic concerning the subject. Recently, Sharon appeared on WWBT 12 News in Virginia and several articles has been published in The Progress-Index and Hopewell Newspapers concerning the coupon work that Sharon is doing.

The information in this book is Sharon's own ideas. This information is compiled from research, hard work, dedication, constant planning, determination and fortitude. Her wisdom is so enduring that the benefits of following her advice and the demonstrated knowledge and understanding you are certain to gain is priceless!

Included in this book is Sharon's straight-talk advice and achievements. You will learn how to cannibalize her ideas into your everyday lifestyle of shopping.

This book is also designed to induce a flow of ideas through your mind, which will generate greater profits for you and your family. So, from Sharon to you...

Happy Couponing!!!

NOTES PAGE

NOTES PAGE

NOTES PAGE

NOTES PAGE

NOTES PAGE